Bible Crossword Puzzle: The New Testament

A Bible-Reading Activity

JinHo, Kim

WESTBOW
PRESS®
A DIVISION OF THOMAS NELSON
& ZONDERVAN

WestBow Press books may be ordered through booksellers or by contacting:

WestBow Press
A Division of Thomas Nelson & Zondervan
1663 Liberty Drive
Bloomington, IN 47403
www.westbowpress.com
1 (866) 928-1240

ISBN: 978-1-5127-1762-4 (sc)

Library of Congress Control Number: 2015917656

Print information available on the last page.

WestBow Press rev. date: 01/07/2016

Bible Crossword Puzzle

- **Matthew 1-5**

- **Across**

① What did Jesus say you were on this earth? (5:13)

② What did the prophets say Jesus would be called? (2:23)

③ What did the angel say to name Joseph's son? (1:21)

- **Down**

① What did the voice from heaven call Jesus? (3:17)

② What kind of kingdom did Jesus say was near? (4:17)

1

Bible Crossword Puzzle

- **Matthew 6-11**

- **Across**

① What did Jesus say will come? (6:10)

② Who was the person sitting at the tax collector's booth and who became a disciple of Jesus? (9:9)

- **Down**

① Whose servant did Jesus heal? (8:13)

② Who is the disciple that was listed after Bartholomew? (10:3)

③ Of what was the stronger foundation made? (7:25)

④ What did Jesus say to put on? (11:29)

Bible Crossword Puzzle

- **Matthew 12-17**

- **Across**

① What kind of seed did Jesus say the kingdom of heaven was like? (13:31)

② With what two things did Jesus give thanks with five loaves? (14:19)

③ Who did Jesus take with James and John? (17:1)

- **Down**

① Over which day did Jesus say the Son of Man is Lord? (12:8)

② What should Jesus' disciples take up? (16:24)

③ For what reason did Jesus say Pharisees and scribes (or teachers of the law) break the command of God? (15:3)

Bible Crossword Puzzle

- **Matthew 18-22**

- **Across**

① What kind of house will the temple be called? (21:13)

② What attitude did Jesus say to have? (18:4)

③ Who did Jesus say let them come to me? (19:14)

- **Down**

① What reason did Jesus come for many? (20:28)

② What should we do to God? (22:37)

Bible Crossword Puzzle

- **Matthew 23-28**

- **Across**

① Who are the people that Jesus condemned with scribes (or teachers of the law) as hypocrites? (23:27)

② How many times did Jesus say Peter will disown me?(26:75)

③ Where is the place Jesus was crucified (27:33)

- **Down**

① What will those who will deceive many people claim for themselves? (24:5)

② What did servants receive from their master? (25:15)

③ To which area of Israel did the disciples go? (28:16)

Bible Crossword Puzzle

- **Mark 1-5**

- **Across**

① What is the name of the synagogue ruler who asked Jesus to heal his daughter? (5:22)

② How many disciples (or apostles) did Jesus appoint? (3:14)

③ What is the insect that John the Baptist ate? (1:6)

- **Down**

① Who did Jesus call as His disciple? (2:14)

② People who are like seed along the path. Who took away the Word which is sown to some of these people? (4:15)

Bible Crossword Puzzle

- **Mark 6-10**

- **Across**

① Who did the woman ask Jesus to heal? (7:26)

② Who is the name of a blind beggar who asked to heal his eyes to Jesus? (10:46)

- **Down**

① What are the disciples allowed to bring for the journey? (6:8)

② What is Peter's answer about who Jesus is? (8:29)

③ What is not quenched in hell? (9:48)

Bible Crossword Puzzle

- **Mark 11-16**

- **Across**

① What did Jesus say to love God with along with all your heart, soul, and mind? (12:30)

② What did Jesus pray to take from Him to the Father? (14:36)

③ Who went with Mary Magdalene, Mary the mother of James to anoint Jesus' body? (16:1)

- **Down**

① What did Jesus sit on? (11:7)

② What must first be preached to all nations in the end of the age? (13:10)

③ Who is the person who tries Jesus? (15:2)

Bible Crossword Puzzle

- **Luke 1- 4**

- **Across**

① What did the angel say to name the son to whom Mary gives birth? (1:31)

② In which bodily form did the Holy Spirit descend on Jesus? (3:22)

- **Down**

① Where was Jesus placed in when he was born? (2:7)

② Whose mother-in-law (or wife's mother) did Jesus heal? (4:38)

Bible Crossword Puzzle

- **Luke 5-9**

- **Across**

① How does the Centurion say his servant will be if Jesus says the word? (7:7)

② After Jesus chose twelve disciples, What did He designate them as? (6:13)

- **Down**

① What did a demon-possessed man say about his name in reply to Jesus' question? (8:30)

② What did Jesus say Simon will catch? (5:10)

③ Did Jesus say what should the disciples shake off if people do not welcome them? (9:5)

Bible Crossword Puzzle

- **Luke 10-14**

- **Across**

① What kind of animals do the disciples seem to be sent among? (10:3)

② What did Jesus say the disciples were worth more than? (12:7)

③ To what kind of seed did Jesus compare the kingdom of God? (13:19)

- **Down**

① In Jesus' teaching about prayer, if we knock on the door, how will it be? (11:9)

② If he humbles himself, how will he be? (14:11)

Bible Crossword Puzzle

- **Luke 15-19**

- **Across**

① To what kind of lost animal did Jesus compare sinners? (15:4)

② Who did a rich man see in Abraham's bosom? (16:23)

③ In a parable about prayer, who kept coming to a judge to get justice? (18:3)

- **Down**

① If our brother repents, what should we do? (17:3)

② Who did Zacchaeus climb up into a sycamore tree to see? (19:4)

Bible Crossword Puzzle

- **Luke 20-24**

- **Across**

① To whom did spies ask Jesus they should pay taxes? (20:22)

② As a sign of the end, which city is surrounded by armies? (21:20)

- **Down**

① Who handed Jesus over to the chief priests? (22:6)

② Who did the crowd ask to do away with Jesus and release to them? (23:18)

③ Where were two disciples going when they met Jesus resurrected? (24:13)

Bible Crossword Puzzle

- **John 1-5**

- **Across**

① In the beginning was the Word. Who was the Word? (1:1)

② What is the name of a town in Samaria where Jesus met a Samaritan woman? (4:5)

③ Who did the man say healed him? (5:15)

- **Down**

① What did Jesus turn into wine? (2:9)

② Who is a man of the Pharisees speaking with Jesus as a teacher who has come from God? (3:1)

Bible Crossword Puzzle

- **John 6-10**

- **Across**

① With what did Jesus compare himself with in the world? (8:12)

② What is the name of the pool where a man blind from his birth was healed? (9:7)

③ With whom does Jesus compare himself? (10:14)

- **Down**

① With what did Jesus compare himself? (6:51)

② What people with the chief priests send officers to arrest Jesus? (7:32)

Bible Crossword Puzzle

- **John 11-15**

Across

① What kind of seed did Jesus mention produces many seeds by dying?(12:24)

② What part of the disciples did Jesus wash? (13:5)

③ With what did Jesus compare the disciples? (15:5)

Down

① What did Jesus say that he was along with the life? (11:25)

② What did Jesus say he was preparing for the disciples ? (14:2)

Bible Crossword Puzzle

- **John 16-21**

- **Across**

① Who does Jesus say has hated the disciples? (17:14)

② Who is the person whose right ear was cut off by Simon Peter? (18:10)

③ Who are those who sit the one at the head, and the other at the feet, where the body of Jesus had lain? (20:12)

- **Down**

① Whom does Jesus say He is with? (16:32)

② What kind of crown did the soldiers place on Jesus' head? (19:2)

③ Who did Jesus ask do you truly love me? (21:16)

Bible Crossword Puzzle

- **Acts 1-5**

- **Across**

① Who is the person who is added to the eleven apostles? (1:26)

② Who is the apostle who healed a man crippled in the name of Jesus Christ of Nazareth? (3:6)

③ Who did the apostles say they must obey rather than men? (5:29)

- **Down**

① Which day were the Apostles and believers filled with the Holy Ghost (or the Holy Spirit)? (2:1)

② What person's name means Son of Encouragement? (4:36)

Bible Crossword Puzzle

- **Acts 6- 10**

- **Across**

① The apostles said they would devote themselves to the ministry of the word and to what else? (6:4)

② What is the name of the person who preaches Christ to a city in Samaria? (8:5)

③ Who met Jesus Christ when he neared Damascus on his journey to persecute believers? (9:4)

- **Down**

① Who is the person who is martyred as he preaches the Gospel before the Sanhedrin?(7:59)

② What is the name of the centurion who invites Peter to his house to be directed by a holy angel?(10:22)

Bible Crossword Puzzle

- **Acts 11-16**

- **Across**

① What were the disciples first called at Antioch? (11:26)

② Did Peter say to whom he was chosen to preach the Gospel? (15:7)

③ Where did a man in Paul's vision ask him to come over to? (16:9)

- **Down**

① What was the church doing for Peter while he was being keeping in prison? (12:5)

② Who did the Holy Ghost (or the Holy Spirit) say to set apart with Saul? (13:2)

③ What building did Paul and Barnabas go into for speaking to Jews and Gentiles? (14:1)

Bible Crossword Puzzle

- **Acts 17-22**

- **Across**

① Who did Paul say Jesus was?(17:3)

② Where did the Jews and Greeks who heard the Word of the Lord from Paul dwell? (19:10)

③ Where did the people plead with Paul not to go? (21:12)

- **Down**

① What eloquent man born at Alexandria, was mighty in the Scriptures? (18:24)

② Who is he who died by falling down in a window because of sleeping as Paul was preaching a long sermon? (20:9)

③ Paul was born in which city in Cilicia?(22:3)

Bible Crossword Puzzle

- **Acts 23 - 28**

- **Across**

① Who are the people who believe there is no resurrection, and neither angels, nor spirits? (23:8)

② To which nation was Paul brought? (27:1)

③ What is the final city where Paul was delivered? (28:16)

- **Down**

① To whom did Tertullus accuse Paul of? (24:3)

② Who is the person who judges Paul? (25:1)

③ Before which king does Paul answer about being accused of the Jews? (26:2)

Bible Crossword Puzzle

- **Romans 1- 5**

- **Across**

① What does the Gospel give to everyone who believes? (1:16)

② What did God show to us through Christ's death? (5:8)

- **Down**

① What will be given to everyone who works good with glory and honor?(2:10)

② What makes humans come short of the glory of God? (3:23)

③ God counted Abraham's faith as what? (4:3)

Bible Crossword Puzzle

- **Romans 6-10**

- **Across**

① What are the wages of sin? (6:23)

② Whose children are counted for the descendants? (9:8)

- **Down**

① What is present with Paul when he would do good? (7:21)

② Neither height, nor depth, nor any other creature can separate us from who? (8:39)

③ What comes by hearing after which hearing comes by the word of God? (10:17)

Bible Crossword Puzzle

- **Romans 11-16**

- **Across**

① Whose apostle does Paul introduce himself as? (11:36)

② Whether we live or die, who do we belong to? (14:8)

③ Which person bestowed much labor on Paul's ministry? (16:6)

- **Down**

① What do believers have to overcome evil with?(12:21)

② Who ordains all powers? (13:1)

③ Who do every one of us have to please for his good? (15:2)

Bible Crossword Puzzle

- **1 Corinthians 1- 5**

- **Across**

① What do we have of Christ's? (2:16)

② What of God's that we are compared with? (3:16)

③ What did Paul say he is present in? (5:3)

- **Down**

① Who does Paul preach is crucified? (1:23)

② The kingdom of God is not in word, but what is the kingdom of God in? (4:20)

Bible Crossword Puzzle

- **1 Corinthians 6-10**

- **Across**

① What of Christ are our bodies compared with? (6:15)

② What does everyone have from God? (7:7)

- **Down**

① What puffs up us? (8:1)

② Which necessity is laid upon Paul to preach? (9:16)

③ Who is the spiritual rock? (10:4)

Bible Crossword Puzzle

- **1 Corinthians 11-16**

- **Across**

① What are diverse in the same Spirit? (12:4)

② Paul says the greatest of three things is love (or charity). What is the one thing other than hope and or charity (or love)? (13:13)

③ By what of God did Paul say I am what I am? (15:10)

- **Down**

① Who is the head of every man? (11:13)

② Paul said we have to seek spiritual gifts for the edifying of what? (14:12)

③ Who did Paul say would not come at this time? (16:12)

Bible Crossword Puzzle

- **2 Corinthians 1- 5**

- **Across**

① Whose name does Paul mention with him at the church at Corinth? (1:1)

② Paul said the spirit gives life, but what did he say kills? (3:6)

- **Down**

① Who do we keep from getting an advantage over us through forgiving? (2:11)

② What of the world had blinded the minds of the people who did not believe? (4:4)

③ In whom can man become a new creature? (5:17)

Bible Crossword Puzzle

- **2 Corinthians 6-9**

- **Across**

① Which day did Paul say is now? (6:2)

② Which kind of giver does God love? (9:7)

- **Down**

① By whose coming did Paul say they were comforted by? (7:6)

② What is Titus to Paul? (8:23)

Bible Crossword Puzzle

- **2 Corinthians 10-13**

- **Across**

① Do they say what is weighty and powerful? (10:10)

② Jesus lives by Christ by the _____ of God. (13:4) (fill in the blank)

- **Down**

① What can Satan be transformed into? (11:14)

② Which number of heaven was a man caught up to? (12:2)

Bible Crossword Puzzle

- **Galatians 1- 6**

- **Across**

① The Gospel Paul preached came through what of Jesus Christ? (1:12)

② Paul said we are the children of promise as who else was? (4:28)

③ Paul said he bears what of the Lord Jesus on his body? (6:17)

- **Down**

① Paul said he was crucified with Christ. Also who did Paul say lives in him? (2:20)

② With whom are those of faith blessed? (3:9)

③ What is the first thing Paul mentioned as the fruit of the Spirit? (5:22)

Bible Crossword Puzzle

- **Ephesians 1- 6**

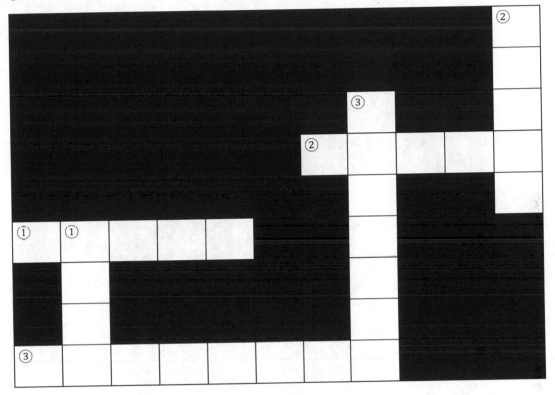

- **Across**

① We have redemption, the forgiveness of sins through what of Jesus Christ? (1:7)

② What are we saved through? (2:8)

③ According to Eph. 4:11, Paul says God gave the following positions in the church: apostles, prophets, evangelists, pastors (or shepherds) and _____. (fill in the blank).

- **Down**

① Paul said we are rooted and grounded in what? (3:17)

② We were sometimes darkness, but now what did we become in the Lord? (5:8)

③ Who should children obey in the Lord? (6:1)

Bible Crossword Puzzle

- **Philippians 1- 4**

- **Across**

① Whether in pretense or in truth, eventually, who or what is preached? (1:18)

② To which tribe did Paul belong? (3:5)

- **Down**

① What should we work out with fear and trembling? (2:12)

② What should we do in the Lord always? (4:4)

Bible Crossword Puzzle

- **Colossians 1- 4**

- **Across**

① Who is the person that Paul describes as a faithful minister of Christ? (1:7)

② Whose word do we let dwell in us richly? (3:16)

- **Down**

① What did we receive Christ Jesus as? (2:6)

② Who is the person that Paul introduces as a beloved brother, a faithful minister, and fellow servant in the Lord? (4:7)

Bible Crossword Puzzle

- **1 Thessalonians 1- 5**

- **Across**

① What other place besides Macedonia were they examples to all the believers? (1:7)

② Did Paul say who tempts us so that our labour is in vain? (3:5)

- **Down**

① Where did Paul say they suffered and were entreated? (2:2)

② From where shall the Lord descend? (4:16)

③ What should we do without ceasing? (5:17)

Bible Crossword Puzzle

- **2 Thessalonians 1- 3**

- **Across**

① Who shows himself to the antichrist by sitting in the temple of God? (2:4)

② Paul says if any would not work, what can they not do? (3:10)

- **Down**

① Who shall reveal the Lord Jesus from heaven? (1:7)

Bible Crossword Puzzle

- **1 Timothy 1- 6**

- **Across**

① To who does Paul send this letter? (1:2)

② If a person speaks lies in hypocrisy, what is seared with a hot iron? (4:2)

③ What does the love of money become the root of all kinds of? (6:10)

- **Down**

① What is Christ Jesus between God and men? (2:5)

② Paul says a certain position in the church has to have the following qualifications: the husband of one wife, and ruling their children and their own houses well.

   What is that position? (3:12)

③ What should we treat an elder (or older) man as? (5:1)

Bible Crossword Puzzle

- **2 Timothy 1-Titus 3**

- **Across**

① Who is the person who refreshed Paul? (1:16)

② What did Paul say he has kept? (4:7)

③ Who is Jesus Christ to us? (2:13)

④ What are we justified by? (3:7)

- **Down**

① To whom should we do our best to show ourselves as a workman that needs not to be ashamed ? (2:15)

② What is being given by inspiration of God, and is profitable for doctrine, for reproof, for correction, and for instruction in righteousness? (3:16)

③ What did God promise to believers before the world began? (1:2)

Bible Crossword Puzzle

- **Philemon 1- Hebrews 6**

- **Across**

① Did Paul say who became his son while he was in chains? (Phm. 1:10)

② Through death, who did Jesus destroy? (2:14)

③ What is living, powerful, and sharper than any two-edged sword piercing even to the division of soul and spirit ? (4:12)

④ Who is the person who offers both gifts and sacrifices for sins? (5:1)

- **Down**

① In times past, God spoke to the fathers by who? (1:1)

② Who built all things? (3:4)

③ Who is an high priest forever? (6:2)

Bible Crossword Puzzle

- **Hebrews 7-13**

- **Across**

① Does the King of Salem mean which king? (7:2)

② It is appointed to men once to die, but after this, what comes? (9:27)

③ What had Jesus Christ offered one sacrifice for forever? (10:12)

④ What kind of sacrifice should we offer to God continually by Jesus? (13:15)

- **Down**

① God said He would make what with the house of Israel and with the house of Judah? (8:8)

② What is it impossible to please God without? (11:6)

③ Who is the author and finisher of our faith? (12:2)

Bible Crossword Puzzle

- **James 1- 5**

- **Across**

① The writer says we should ask God for what? (1:5)

② God resists the proud, but to whom does God give grace? (4:6)

- **Down**

① Does the writer say what is perfect by works? (2:22)

② What is full of deadly poison and no man can tame? (3:8)

③ What activity should someone who is afflicted engage in? (5:13)

Bible Crossword Puzzle

- **1 Peter 1-5**

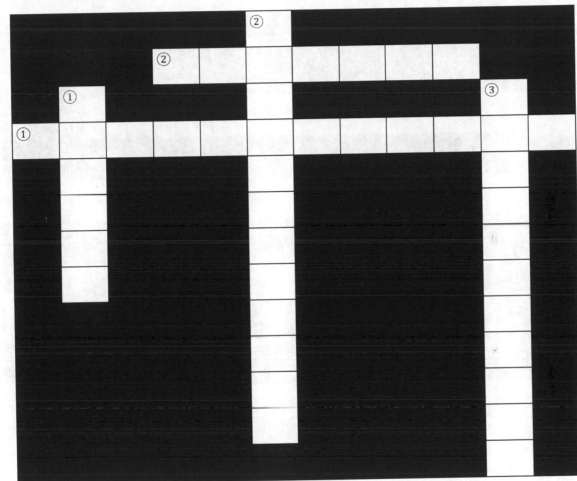

- **Across**

① We born again by what? (1:23)

② What emotion does Peter tell you not to feel when you suffer as a Christian? (4:16)

- **Down**

① Who suffered for us to leave us an example? (2:21)

② To whose prayers are God's ears open? (3:12)

③ With shat does Peter compare the devil? (5:8)

43

Bible Crossword Puzzle

- **2 Peter 1- 1 John 2**

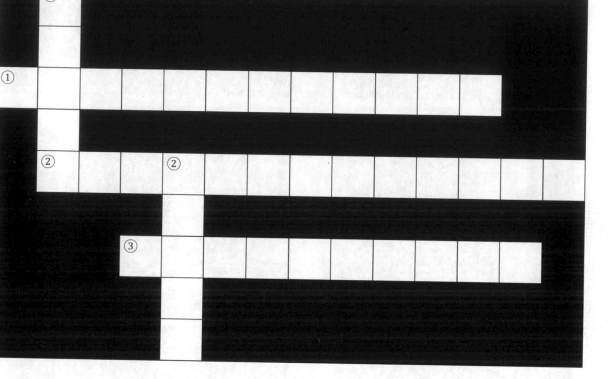

- **Across**

① God wants us to become partakers of what? (1:4)

② Who privily shall bring in damnable heresies? (2:1)

③ Who denies the Father and the Son? (1Jn 2:22)

- **Down**

① What will the day of the Lord come in the night as? (3:10)

② What should we confess for forgiveness from God who is faithful and just? (1Jn 1:9)

Bible Crossword Puzzle

- **1John 3 - Jude 1**

- **Across**

① John says someone who commits sin belongs to who? (1Jn 3:8)

② John says that when we walk after his commandments, it is what? (2Jn 1:6)

③ What is the name of the archangel recorded in Jude 1:9? (Jude 1:9)

- **Down**

① John says love belongs to who? (1 Jn 4:7)

② We should ask any thing to God according to what? (1Jn 5:14)

③ Who is the person that John describes as the person who loves to have the preeminence among them? (3Jn 1:9)

Bible Crossword Puzzle

- **Revelation 1-6**

- **Across**

① What did the Lord has in his right hand? (1:16)

② Whose root has prevailed to open the book? (5:5)

③ What kind of animal did He sit on? (6:2)

- **Down**

① Which church left its first love? (2:1,4)

② Which church has a little strength and has kept the Lord's Word and has not denied the Lord's name? (3:7,8)

③ What are the twenty-four people? (4:10)

Bible Crossword Puzzle

- **Revelation 7 – 12**

- **Across**

① Which 144,000 people were sealed? (7:4)

② What did John see come down from heaven? (10:1)

③ What was cast out? it is the old serpent called the devil, and Satan. (12:9)

- **Down**

① What was given to seven angels? (8:2)

② There came out of the smoke, and what came upon the earth? (9:3)

③ What made the tenth part of the city fall? (11:13)

Bible Crossword Puzzle

- **Revelation 13 – 17**

- **Across**

① What did the dragon give his power to? (13:4)

② Who performs to pour seven bowls of the wrath of God upon the earth? (16:1)

③ What do ten horns mean? (17:12)

- **Down**

① What shouldn't any man receive on his forehead, or in his hand? (14:9)

② What did seven angels have? (15:1)

Bible Crossword Puzzle

- **Revelation 18 – 22**

- **Across**

① Another angel said what is fallen? (18:2)

② How many years will those who have part in the first resurrection reign with Christ? (20:6)

- **Down**

① The fine linen is whose righteousness? (19:8)

② What did John see coming down from God out of heaven? (21:2)

③ On either side of the river, what was there? (22:2)

Answer Key

P.N.		across		down	P.N.		across		down
1	1	salt	1	son	25	1	gentiles	1	good
	2	Nazareth	2	heaven		2	Lord	2	God
	3	Jesus				3	Mary	3	neighbor
2	1	kingdom	1	Centurion	26	1	mind	1	Christ
	2	Matthew	2	Thomas		2	temlpe	2	power
			3	Rock		3	spirit		
			4	Yoke	27	1	members	1	knowledge
3	1	mustard	1	Sabbath		2	gift	2	gospel
	2	Fish	2	cross				3	Christ
	3	Peter	3	tradition	28	1	gifts	1	Christ
4	1	prayer	1	ransom		2	faith	2	church
	2	humble	2	Love		3	grace	3	apollos
	3	children			29	1	timothy	1	satan
5	1	Pharisees	1	Christ		2	letter	2	God
	2	three	2	talents				3	Christ
	3	Golgotha	3	Galilee	30	1	salvation	1	titus
6	1	Jairus	1	Levi		2	cheerful	2	partner
	2	twelve	2	Satan	31	1	letters	1	angel
	3	locusts				2	power	2	third
7	1	daughter	1	Staff	32	1	revelation	1	Christ
	2	Bartimaeus	2	Christ		2	isaac	2	abraham
			3	fire		3	marks	3	love
8	1	Strength	1	colt	33	1	blood	1	love
	2	Cup	2	Gospel		2	faith	2	light
	3	Salome	3	Pilate		3	teachers	3	parents
9	1	Jesus	1	manger	34	1	Christ	1	salvation
	2	dove	2	Simon		2	benjamin	2	rejoice
10	1	healed	1	Legion	35	1	epaphras	1	Lord
	2	apostles	2	Men		2	Christ	2	tychicus
			3	dust	36	1	achaia	1	philippi
11	1	wolves	1	opened		2	tempter	2	heaven
	2	sparrows	2	exalted				3	prayer
	3	mustard			37	1	God	1	angels
12	1	sheep	1	Forgive		2	eat		
	2	Lazarus	2	Jesus	38	1	timothy	1	mediator
	3	widow				2	conscienc	2	deacon
13	1	Caesar	1	Judas		3	evil	3	father
	2	Jerusalem	2	Barabbas	39	1	onesiphorus	1	God
			3	Emmaus		2	faith	2	allscripture
14	1	God	1	water		3	savior	3	eternallife
	2	Sychar	2	Nicodemus		4	grace		
	3	Jesus			40	1	onesimus	1	prophets
15	1	light	1	Bread		2	devil	2	God
	2	Siloam	2	Pharisees		3	thewordofGod	3	Jesus

P.N.		across		down
	3	shepherd		
16	1	wheat	1	resurrection
16	2	feet	2	place
16	3	branches		
17	1	world	1	Father
17	2	Malchus	2	thorns
17	3	angels	3	Simon
18	1	matthias	1	pentecost
18	2	peter	2	barnabas
18	3	God		
19	1	prayer	1	stephen
19	2	philip	2	cornelius
19	3	saul		
20	1	christians	1	prayer
20	2	gentiles	2	barnabas
20	3	macedonia	3	synagogue
21	1	christ	1	apollos
21	2	asia	2	eutychus
21	3	jerusalem	3	tarsus
22	1	sadducees	1	felix
22	2	italy	2	festus
22	3	rome	3	agrippa
23	1	salvation	1	peace
23	2	love	2	sin
23			3	righteousness
24	1	death	1	evil
24	2	promise	2	God
24			3	faith

P.N.		across		down
	4	highpriest		
41	1	peace	1	newcovenant
41	2	judgment	2	faith
41	3	sins	3	Jesus
41	4	praise		
42	1	wisdom	1	faith
42	2	thehumble	2	tongue
42			3	prayer
43	1	thewordofGod	1	Christ
43	2	ashamed	2	therighteous
43			3	roaringlion
44	1	divinenature	1	thief
44	2	falseteachers	2	sins
44	3	antichrist		
45	1	thedevil	1	God
45	2	love	2	hiswil
45	3	michael	3	diotreph
46	1	sevenstars	1	ephesus
46	2	david	2	philadelphia
46	3	horse	3	elder
47	1	israel	1	trumpet
47	2	angel	2	locusts
47	3	greatdragon	3	earthquake
48	1	thebeast	1	mark
48	2	sevenangels	2	sevenplagues
48	3	tenkings		
49	1	babylon	1	saints
49	2	onethousand	2	newjerusalem
49	3	thetreeoflife		

Bible Reading Chart

NAME :

Matt	1	2	3	4	5	6	7	8	9	10	11	12	13	14	15	16	17	18	19	20
	21	22	23	24	25	26	27	28												
Mk	1	2	3	4	5	6	7	8	9	10	11	12	13	14	15	16				
Lk	1	2	3	4	5	6	7	8	9	10	11	12	13	14	15	16	17	18	19	20
	21	22	23	24																
Jn	1	2	3	4	5	6	7	8	9	10	11	12	13	14	15	16	17	18	19	20
	21																			
Acts	1	2	3	4	5	6	7	8	9	10	11	12	13	14	15	16	17	18	19	20
	21	22	23	24	25	26	27	28												
Rom	1	2	3	4	5	6	7	8	9	10	11	12	13	14	15	16				
1 Cor	1	2	3	4	5	6	7	8	9	10	11	12	13	14	15	16				
2 Cor	1	2	3	4	5	6	7	8	9	10	11	12	13							
Gal	1	2	3	4	5	6														
Eph	1	2	3	4	5	6														
Phlp	1	2	3	4																
Col	1	2	3	4																
1 Thes	1	2	3	4	5															
2 Thes	1	2	3																	
1 Tim	1	2	3	4	5	6														
2 Tim	1	2	3	4																
Titus	1	2	3																	
Phil	1																			
Heb	1	2	3	4	5	6	7	8	9	10	11	12	13							
Jam	1	2	3	4	5															
1 Pt	1	2	3	4	5															
2 Pt	1	2	3																	
1 Jn	1	2	3	4	5															
2 Jn	1																			
3 Jn	1																			
Jude	1																			
Rev	1	2	3	4	5	6	7	8	9	10	11	12	13	14	15	16	17	18	19	20
	21	22																		

About the Author

For more than two decades, he worked with dedication as a Sunday school teacher, a children's minister, a youth pastor, a Bible teacher, and an assistant pastor. He especially holds a deep interest in youth ministry and Christian education.

He received a master of arts in Christian education (MACE) from Southwestern Baptist Theological Seminary. He currently is a PhD candidate in student ministry and family ministry in Southwestern Baptist Theological Seminary.